Dear Friend,

I used to be a really, really bad homeschooler.

Now, you are wondering, "Does she think I'm a bad homeschooler?" But, no, I already know for sure that you are not a bad homeschooler. You're actually a very, very good homeschool mom. You should feel pride.

What made me a bad homeschool mom? I was so, so stinkin' prideful. I thought I knew everything. My friend Pam tried to help me, and I politely said, "No, thank you." She gave me catalogs and magazines and books to look at, and I brushed them aside. "I know all of that," I scoffed.

Boy, was I stupid.

(Yep, I said the word stupid. It totally applies in this case.)

It took me years and years of mistakes and frustrations before I realized the sober truth:

None of us are perfect at homeschooling.

But we are great at what matters.

- Loving our children
- Sacrificing for their education
- Searching for answers
- Keeping our children alive

And that's how I know you are such a great homeschooler. You know that, you keep going, and you are trying right now – today – to learn more, find more, experience more.

You rock.

I do not know everything there is to know about homeschooling. Who does? There are a lot of people who know a lot of things about homeschooling, and I knew a little, and there's books that have a ton of information … so I thought I'd try to put it all together in one place.

Everything You Need to Know About Homeschooling.

I'm going to tell you the truth: I don't even remember a lot that's in the book. It's too huge. I wrote it all down so I would know where to find the information I needed. Then I thought maybe you might like to have it all in one place, too.

And once it was all over, the conversations with experts, the research, the writing, the editing, the consultations with first readers, when it was all over, I needed to take a breath. A deep breath.

Then I wanted to think. To meditate. To journal. To pray.

So here's what I'm using. I hope you can use it, too, to find the best way for you and your family.

Remember,

teach the way you teach best for the way your child learns best.

That's all there is.

Your new friend and compatriot in this great journey,

Lea Ann

177

54

49

59

90

Introduction

why I'm here

Why are you reading this book and doing this study? What is on your mind, what is bothering you, what questions do you have? Get it all out here. Then at the end, see if you feel better about it all.

homeschool journey

In the introduction, I shared with you how I didn't want to homeschool ... and why I do now. What has been your journey to homeschooling? Are you still thinking about it, in the middle of it, questioning your decision? Write out your thoughts about where you are in your homeschool journey and where you hope to be someday.

Can homeschooling be different from the norm? I'm here to tell you that *homeschooling must be different.*

Your homeschool must be different from mine, from your friend's, from the expert at the convention's. Your homeschool must be different from that of the previous generation, from that of the boxed set, from that of the how-to guide. Your homeschool must be as different as the family you lead. Because each child is uniqe, each family culture is unique, and each day has its own unique challenges.

Everything You Need to Know About Homeschooling, page 3

YOUR
WHY

THE REASONS YOU HOMESCHOOL
Chapter 1

FAITH

Instill values, worldview, morals you want to pass on to your child.

ACADEMICS

Let your child take off with her talents and concentrate on her difficulties.

CULTURE

Teach your student of his past, his present, and his future life in light of his unique heritage

RELATIONSHIPS

Build your family with closer relationships through shared experiences.

Chapter 1
Finding Your Homeschool Why

my own why

Your homeschool is unique, just like your family is unique. So just for you personally, why do you homeschool? Not just the "this is what I'm supposed to say" answer, but what is your actual, deep-down motivation? Write it here. No judgements.

my real priorities

Now look at those reasons. Are they the priorities you want to have? Do you wish you would have more? Are you living consistently with your purpose? Write down your own thoughts and feelings about your reasons.

my real life

Finally, consider your why in daily life. What will this look like in the day-to-day?

I can do all things through
him who strengthens me.
Philippians 4:13

Chapter 2

Get Ready for the Questions

objections

What are relatives, friends, and acquaintances saying about homeschooling? What are their questions, their objections, their judgements?

questions

What are your own questions, fears, and hesitations? What are your secret doubts?

The more I need to explain or even defend homeschooling, the more I reaffirm my own commitment. Explaining my own *why* and how we live this life helps me recognize God's plan and provision in our lives. I know God wants me to homeschool, and now I'm *bold* to tell you so.

answers

What are some reassuring answers you found in chapter 2? How will these change your answers to others and answers to your own fears?

prayers

Write out your prayer to God, giving him your fears of others and of homeschooling.

practical

What are small, practical ways you can in faith live out your new confidence?

prove it

What are ways you are already living out your homeschool beliefs?

how I socialize

why I am the best teacher for my child

Not by might, not by power,
but by my Spirit,
says the Lord of hosts.
Zechariah 4:6

what are the legal requirements of my state

Look on hslda.com or contact your local support group

what is my local support group

how we will meet our financial needs

how our family will adjust

Chapter 3
Ready, Set, Go

So much will change throughout the year, so just relax and go with it. Nothing is set in stone. You can change style, materials, schedule - anything. Just look at this as a trial-and-error and enjoy the process.

- Everything There is to Know About Homeschooling, page 40

my first day of the year

Whether you are a new or experienced homeschool mom, don't make a schedule for your first day. Just go for two or three activities or goals to warm up you and your child.

fun ways to celebrate the first day

my first week of the year.

Just like your first day, you don't need a strict schedule. What are a few goals for these days?

Minimalist school supplies

The few things you need for a relaxing first day. For more detailed information about in-depth teaching, curriculum and supplies, see part 3.

- [ ] pencils
- [ ] paper
- [ ] Bible or Bible story book

- [ ] Simple math book or workbook
- [ ] Simple grammar book or workbook
- [ ] Library card
- [ ] Snacks

- [ ]
- [ ]
- [ ]

- [ ]
- [ ]
- [ ]

- [ ]
- [ ]
- [ ]

- [ ]
- [ ]
- [ ]

- [ ]
- [ ]

- [ ]

Starting out: early learning

If this is your first year, start with just a few things. Then see chapter 10 for more ideas.

- [ ] pencils and crayons
- [ ] paper
- [ ] Bible or Bible story book
- [ ] Small toys or snacks to count
- [ ] Simple phonics program
- [ ] Flashcards, letter magnets, or other games
- [ ] Library card
- [ ] Snacks
- [ ]
- [ ]
- [ ]
- [ ]
- [ ]
- [ ]
- [ ]
- [ ]
- [ ]
- [ ]
- [ ]
- [ ]
- [ ]
- [ ]
- [ ]

Starting out: elementary and middle school

If this is your first year, start with just a few things. Then see chapter 11 for more ideas.

- [ ] pencils
- [ ] paper
- [ ] Bible or Bible story book
- [ ] Grammar workbook
- [ ] Math workbook
- [ ] Library card
- [ ] Snacks
- [ ]
- [ ]
- [ ]
- [ ]
- [ ]
- [ ]
- [ ]
- [ ]
- [ ]
- [ ]
- [ ]
- [ ]
- [ ]
- [ ]
- [ ]

Starting out: high school

If this is your first year, start with just a few things. Then see chapter 13 for more ideas

- [ ] pencils
- [ ] paper

- [ ] Bible
- [ ] Grammar, literature, or writing curriculum
- [ ] Math curriculum

- [ ] Science curriculum
- [ ] History curriculum

- [ ] Snacks
- [ ]
- [ ]
- [ ]
- [ ]
- [ ]
- [ ]
- [ ]
- [ ]
- [ ]
- [ ]
- [ ]
- [ ]
- [ ]
- [ ]
- [ ]

If this is your first year, start with just a few things. Then see chapter 13 for more ideas

Chapter 4
We Aren't in School Anymore

Begin having students read directions aloud and try the first steps.

Assign weekly instead of daily.

Let her grade homework,
but you grade tests.

Check progress regularly.

Set goals and rewards.

Use a timer to set end times for subjects.

Let her choose where and when
she studies.

Encourage her to read and research
answers and try to solve the problem
before coming to you for help.

Hold her accountable for work,
not how much time she spends.

Tips for fostering independent learning.

my unique homeschool

List some ways that your homeschool is different from institutional school.

my deschooling

List some ways you can help your child relax and you can build learning relationships.

HOW TO BE A
Good Teacher

Focus on *success*, not grades.

Know how you teach best.

Teach the way your child learns best.

Only change *one small thing* at a time.

Remain available for help.

Admit you don't know everything.

Help your student find the answer.

Remember *why* you teach.

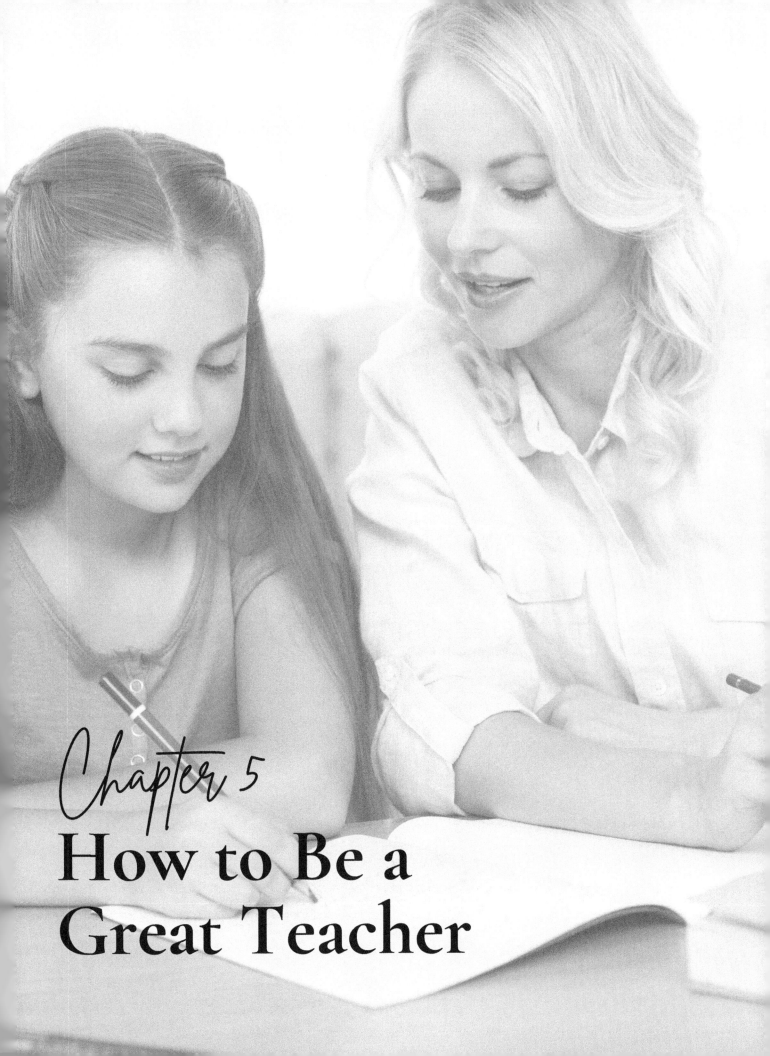

Chapter 5
How to Be a
Great Teacher

my strengths

Think about what makes you a great mom. Your compassion? Your intuition? Your patience? Your love of books? Your enthusiasm for crafts? Your interest in science? List your strengths and interests. These make you a great teacher, too!

my secret weapons

How can you get help? Online resources? Co-op? Tutoring? Brainstorm some ideas here.

Look ahead

to where you would like your student to be in each subject. Envision not what the curriculum covers, what the final test is over, what the publisher's scope and sequence describes. Nope. You are the teacher, my friend. And you know what your child can and should learn through the coming year.

You are in charge of this homeschooling

not the bossy curriculum.

my student's specific academic goals

List just a few things you want to cover this year. Make it specific, not textbook. Instead of "finish Math 5" think about "master long division and understand fractions." Instead of "complete American history" try "read 10 biographies and tell the story of the American Revolution."

my student's specific academic goals

List just a few things you want to cover this year. Make it specific, not textbook. Instead of "finish Math 5" think about "master long division and understand fractions." Instead of "complete American history" try "read 10 biographies and tell the story of the American Revolution."

my student's specific academic goals

List just a few things you want to cover this year. Make it specific, not textbook. Instead of "finish Math 5" think about "master long division and understand fractions." Instead of "complete American history" try "read 10 biographies and tell the story of the American Revolution."

my student's specific academic goals

List just a few things you want to cover this year. Make it specific, not textbook. Instead of "finish Math 5" think about "master long division and understand fractions." Instead of "complete American history" try "read 10 biographies and tell the story of the American Revolution."

MOST IMPORTANT GOALS

THE FEW THINGS THAT MAKE YOU A SUCCESSFUL TEACHER

see more in chapter 5

- faithfulness in your calling

- strengthened relationship with God

- life skills

- service

- love for others

my student's specific life goals

What are emotional, mental, and spiritual goals for this year?

my student's specific life goals

What are emotional, mental, and spiritual goals for this year?

my student's specific life goals
What are emotional, mental, and spiritual goals for this year?

my student's specific life goals

What are emotional, mental, and spiritual goals for this year?

Commit your work to the Lord and your *plans* will be established.

Prov. 16:3

break it down

How can you specifically work on these academic and life goals this month?

break it down

How can you specifically work on these academic and life goals this month?

break it down

How can you specifically work on these academic and life goals this month?

break it down

How can you specifically work on these academic and life goals this month?

Lesson Plan Templates

Your student is often engaged in her studies.

You overcome difficulties over time.

You are finding your homeschool style.

Your student is making gradual progress.

Your student applies his learning to other subjects.

You are starting to adapt to your student's learning style.

SIGNS YOUR HOMESCHOOL IS GOING
Well

Others remark on your student's growth.

Your student achieves modest test scores.

Your student graduates.

Your student answers strangers' quizzes admirably.

Your student won't exhibit all these signs, but you may find one or two to encourage you. More affirmation and encouragement in chapter 14

Your student finds a job.

subject:

Monday

Tuesday

Wednesday

Thursday

notes

Weekly Goals

ENGLISH

MATH

HISTORY

SCIENCE

ELECTIVE

ELECTIVE

Week of:

Monday	Tuesday	Wednesday	Thursday	Friday

Week of:

Monday	Tuesday	Wednesday	Thursday	Friday

Chapter 6
The Way You Teach Best

Textbook

What are parts you like?

What are parts you would change?

> Remember that you are in charge of your child's education. It is not the book that educates: rather you are educating your child. Confidently tailor your child's learning for his needs.
>
> --*Everything You Need to Know About Homeschooling,* page 83

classical homeschooling

What are parts you like?

What are parts you would change?

> Do your best to present
> yourself to God as one
> approved, a worker who
> has no need to be ashamed,
> rightly handling the word
> of truth.
> -- 2 Timothy 2:15

Charlotte Mason homeschooling

What are parts you like?

What are parts you would change?

The most important part
of education is to give the
children the knowledge of
God.

-- Charlotte Mason

Montessori homeschooling

What are parts you like?

What are parts you would change?

Teach the child
how to learn.

-

-- *Everything You Need to*
Know About Homeschooling,
page 98

unschooling

What are parts you like?

What are parts you would change?

Allowing children to
practice freedom prepares
them for a lifetime of
living under God's love
and care.

*-- Everything You Need to
Know About Homeschooling,*
page 106

unit studies

What are parts you like?

What are parts you would change?

co-ops

What are parts you like?

What are parts you would change?

online learning

What are parts you like?

What are parts you would change?

other methods

What are parts you like?

What are parts you would change?

my own way

How do you combine these ideas to how you teach best?

> There is no one right way
> to homeschool ... teach the
> way you teach best.
>
> *-- Everything You Need to*
> *Know About Homeschooling,*
> page 116

Chapter 7
How Children Learn

VARK learning for you

What VARK style is most like you?

How does your VARK style affect your teaching?

VARK learning for your student

What VARK style is most like your student?

How does his VARK style affect his learning?

VARK learning for your student

What VARK style is most like your student?

How does his VARK style affect his learning?

VARK learning for your student

What VARK style is most like your student?

How does his VARK style affect his learning?

VARK learning ideas

What VARK style changes do you want to make to your homeschooling?

We don't homeschool for ourselves, we homeschool for *God.*

Gregorc learning for you

What Gregorc quadrant is most like you?

How does your Gregorc quadrant affect your teaching?

Gregorc learning for your student

What Gregorc quadrant is most like your student?

How does his Gregorc quadrant affect his learning?

Gregorc learning for your student

What Gregorc quadrant is most like your student?

How does his Gregorc quadrant affect his learning?

Gregorc learning for your student

What Gregorc quadrant is most like your student?

How does his Gregorc quadrant affect his learning?

Gregorc learning for your student

What Gregorc quadrant is most like your student?

How does his Gregorc quadrant affect his learning?

Gregorc learning ideas

What Gregorc model changes do you want to make to your homeschooling?

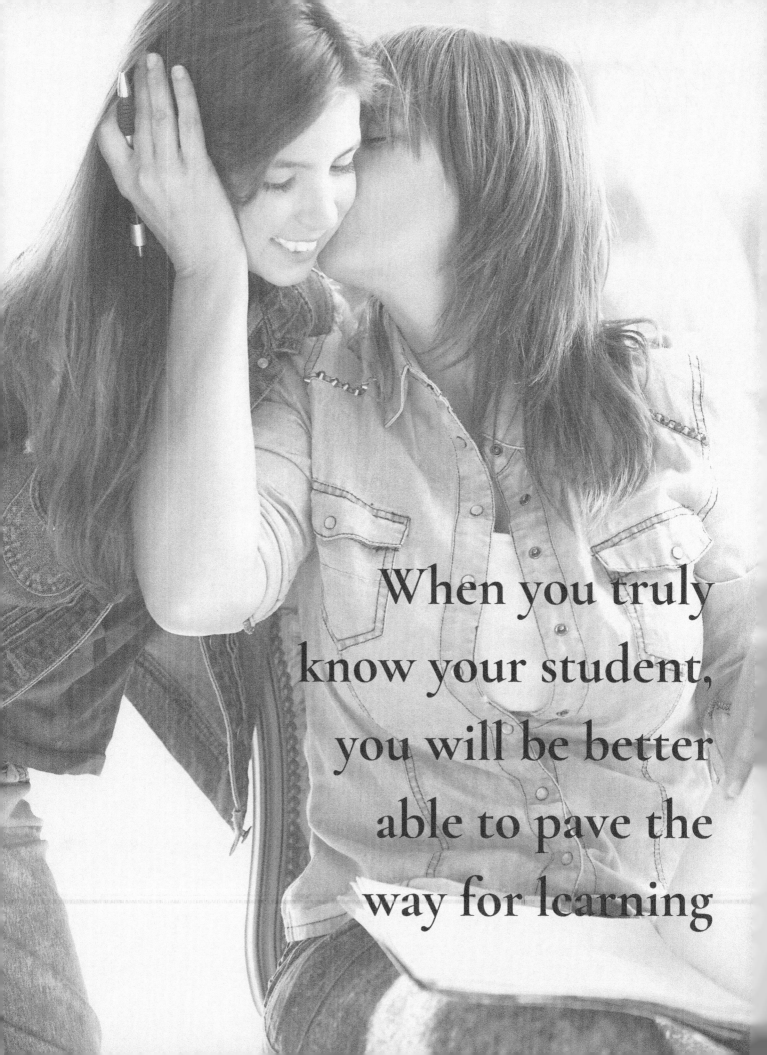

When you truly know your student, you will be better able to pave the way for learning

Willis and Hodson learning for you

What disposition is most like you?

How does your disposition affect your teaching?

Willis and Hodson learning for your student

What disposition is most like your student?

How does his disposition affect his learning?

Willis and Hodson learning for your student

What disposition is most like your student?

How does his disposition affect his learning?

Willis and Hodson learning for your student

What disposition is most like your student?

How does his disposition affect his learning?

Willis and Hodson learning for your student

What disposition is most like your student?

How does his disposition affect his learning?

Willis and Hosdon learning ideas

What learning process changes do you want to make to your homeschooling?

Dunn and Dunn aspects of learning for you

What are aspects of your learning in these areas:

environmental

emotional

sociological

What are aspects of your learning in these areas:

physiological

psychological

How do your preferences affect your teaching?

Dunn and Dunn aspects of learning for your student

What are aspects of your student's learning in these areas:

environmental

emotional

sociological

What are aspects of his learning in these areas:

physiological

psychological

How do her preferences affect her learning?

Dunn and Dunn aspects of learning for your student

What are aspects of your student's learning in these areas?

environmental

emotional

sociological

What are aspects of her learning in these areas:

physiological

psychological

How do her preferences affect her learning?

Dunn and Dunn aspects of learning for your student

What are aspects of your student's learning in these areas?

environmental

emotional

sociological

What are aspects of her learning in these areas:

physiological

psychological

How do her preferences affect her learning?

Dunn and Dunn learning ideas

What learning preference changes do you want to make to your homeschooling?

talents

What are some special abilities you and your child possess?

talents

What are some special abilities you and your child possess?

putting it all together

What are some ideas you want to try in your homeschool?

putting it all together

What are some ideas you want to try in your homeschool?

putting it all together

What are some ideas you want to try in your homeschool?

Chapter 8
Books and Stuff

curriculum

What style curriculum (textbook, boxed, online, digital, real books) suits you best for each subject and each student?

curriculum

What style curriculum (textbook, boxed, online, digital, real books) suits you best for each subject and each student?

curriculum

What style curriculum (textbook, boxed, online, digital, real books) suits you best for each subject and each student?

curriculum

What style curriculum (textbook, boxed, online, digital, real books) suits you best for each subject and each student?

choosing my materials

What products and curriculum do you want to preview? Can you borrow it from a friend or find a sample online?

We sometimes equate *homeschooling* with *curriculum*. We put a lot of pressure on ourselves to choose the correct books so we will "homeschool right." Over time, however, we begin to realize books don't teach children -

parents teach children

Everything You Need to Know About Homeschooling, page 147

choosing my materials

What products and curriculum do you want to preview? Can you borrow it for a friend or find a sample online?

Chapter 9
What Grade Are We In?

nature

What academic and mental traits has your student inherited? How is his physical growth affecting his learning?

nurture

What events in the child's past affect his learning? What about the present?

past learning

What has been your student's past academic progress? How is that affecting his current work?

intelligence

Which intelligences (section 9.2.4) does your child exhibit?

disabilities

Does your child exhibit symptoms of a learning disability? Or are there areas she struggles with?

Chapter 10
Early Learning

development

What milestones in character is your early learner reaching?

What milestones in growth is your early learner reaching?

development

What milestones mentally is your early learner reaching?

What milestones socially and emotionally is your early learner reaching?

Sample Routine: Early Learning

Mommy time

breakfast

chores

playtime

Bible story

phonics: 10 minutes

number time: 10 minutes

snack time

activity/craft time

playtime

lunch

read aloud

rest time

play

academics

What is your child working on this year in Bible?

What is your child working on this year in reading?

academics

What is your child working on this year in fine motor skills?

What is your child working on this year in writing?

academics

What is your child working on this year in math?

What is your child working on this year in memorization?

academics

What is your child working on this year in other subjects?

academics

What is your child working on this year in other subjects?

getting ready for elementary

What milestones can you just sit back and wait on?

What milestones are you waiting for to move on to elementary?

Chapter 11
Elementary

development

What milestones in character is your elementary student reaching?

What milestones in growth is your elementary student reaching?

development

What milestones mentally is your elementary student reaching?

What milestones socially and emotionally is your elementary student reaching?

Sample Routine: Elementary

see chapter 11

Mommy time

breakfast

chores

Bible time

reading: 20 minutes

grammar: 20 minutes

snack time

math: 30 minutes

history or science: 30 minutes

elective: 20 minutes

play time

lunch

read aloud

quiet play or reading

play

academics

What is your student working on this year in Bible?

What is your student working on this year in reading?

academics

What is your student working on this year in writing?

What is your student working on this year in spelling?

academics

What is your student working on this year in grammar?

What is your student working on this year in math?

academics

What is your student working on this year in memorization?

What is your student working on this year in science?

academics

What is your student working on this year in history and social studies?

What is your student working on this year in other electives?

getting ready for middle school

What milestones can you just sit back and wait on?

What milestones are you waiting for to move on to middle school?

Chapter 12
Middle School

development

What milestones in character is your middle school student reaching?

What milestones in growth is your middle school student reaching?

development

What milestones mentally is your middle school student reaching?

What milestones socially and emotionally is your middle school student reaching?

Sample Routine: Middle School

Mommy time

breakfast

chores

Bible

literature/grammar: 30 minutes

snack time

math: 30 minutes

history/science: 30 minutes

independent work

electives: 30 minutes

lunch

read aloud

quiet reading/homework/playing

play time/hobbies

academics

What is your student working on this year in Bible?

What is your student working on this year in English?

academics

What is your student working on this year in math?

What is your student working on this year in science?

academics

What is your student working on this year in history and social studies?

What is your student working on this year in electives?

What is your student working on this year in history and social studies?

getting ready for high school

What milestones can you just sit back and wait on?

What milestones are you waiting for to move on to high school?

Chapter 13

High School

development

What milestones in character is your high school student reaching?

What milestones in growth is your high school student reaching?

development

What milestones mentally is your high school student reaching?

What milestones socially and emotionally is your high school student reaching?

Sample Routine: High School

see chapter 13

Mommy time	independent work: 30-45 minutes
breakfast	relax: 30 minutes
chores	lunch
Bible	read aloud
review work together: 30 minutes	quiet homework/reading
independent work: 30-45 minutes	questions on homework
snack time	play/hobbies

academics

What is your student working on this year in Bible?

What is your student working on this year in English?

academics

What is your student working on this year in math?

What is your student working on this year in science?

academics

What is your student working on this year in history and social studies?

What is your student working on this year in physical education?

academics

What is your student working on this year in other electives?

academics

What is your student working on this year in other electives?

getting ready for graduation

What milestones does your teen need to meet to graduate? How will you meet them?

Chapter 14
The Dangers of Homeschooling

dangers within

Which dangers do you struggle with?

dangers within

Which dangers do you struggle with?

dangers within

What can you do to overcome these dangers?

dangers within

What can you do to overcome these dangers?

AVOID BURNOUT

Read more in chapter 14

Burnout *will* come because we are weak human beings. We forget - God, remind us - that we truly *cannot do this of ourselves.* God did not call us to homeschool because we are all-powerful and all-knowing.

God called us because *he is.*

When we try to homeschool in our own strength, in our own wisdom, we quickly find ourselves insufficient for the task. When we, instead, lean on him for provision, we find his grace. But as humans, we still do try to work this all out on our own. There is such a fine line between *doing our best* and *doing it ourselves.* This is why we need to recognize our tendency to burn out, to be "weary of doing good" and to plan for refreshment. We need to consciously create opportunities to return to God's grace, to his perfect rest.

- plan for daily and seasonal breaks

- get tutors or co-ops for teaching

- find a change of scenery

- exercise regularly

- sleep well

- eat healthy

- spend time with friends

- simplify your teaching or curriculum

- spend relaxing time with family

- say no to other responsibilities and activities

- keep your spiritual and emotional health a priority

comparison dangers

Who or what are you tempted to compare your homeschooling to? How can you ensure you are homeschooling your unique way for your own unique family?

relationship dangers

What relationships are strained in your family and relationships right now? What are concrete steps you can take to build these up?

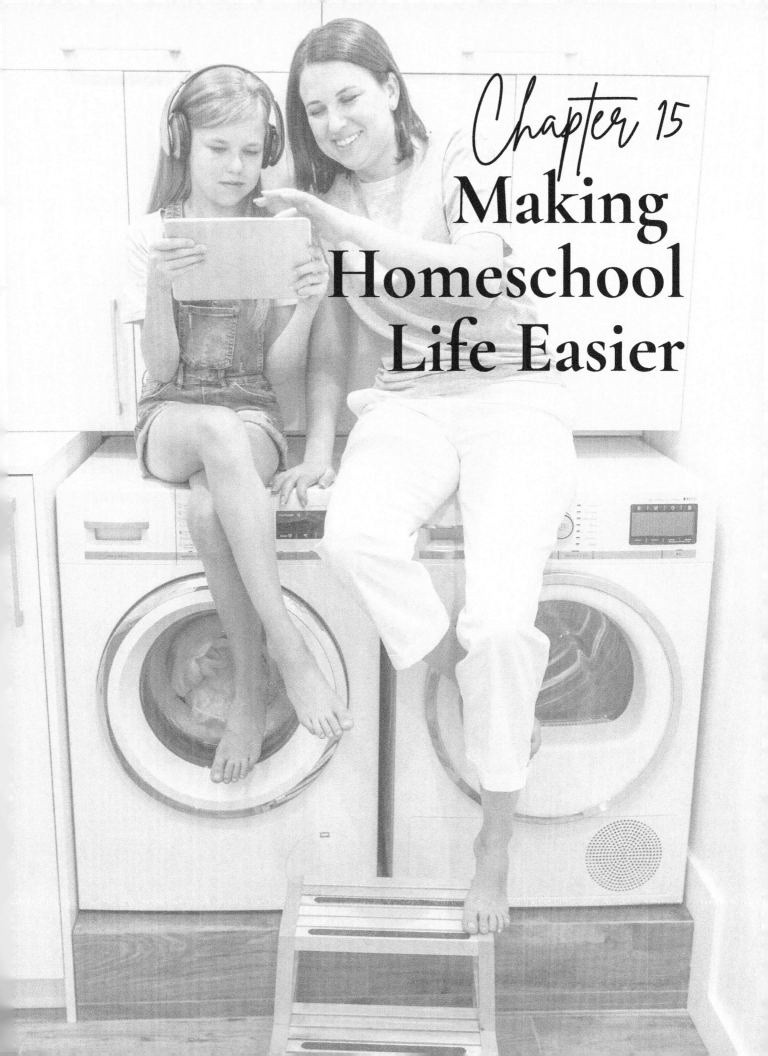

Chapter 15
Making Homeschool Life Easier

self-care

Read 15.1 and 15.2 What ideas do you have to take care of yourself physically, mentally, and emotionally better?

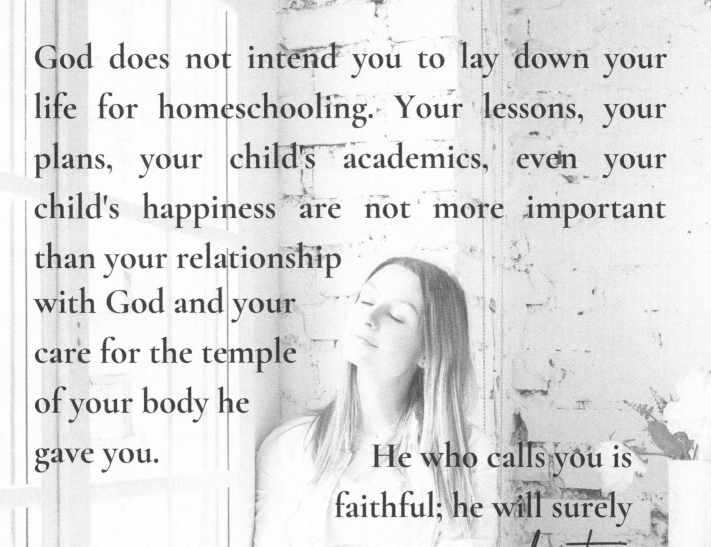

God does not intend you to lay down your life for homeschooling. Your lessons, your plans, your child's academics, even your child's happiness are not more important than your relationship with God and your care for the temple of your body he gave you.

He who calls you is faithful; he will surely *do it.*

1 Thes. 5:24

Everything You Need to Know About Homeschooling, page 457

family care

How can you calm relationships and encurage your child?

Sample Routine: Multiple Children

Mommy time

breakfast

chores

Bible: 20 minutes

Assignment discussion: 20 minutes

reading with littles/older ones work independently: 20 minutes

youngest plays/colors/works with manipulatives

one at a time work with students while youngest plays: 20 min each

snack time

math with youngest

work through older children

group lesson: history/science/ elective

lunch

read aloud

youngest rest time/work with older

quiet reading for everyone

play

Sample Routine: Multiple Children including Teens

same as before,
but teens help with younger
during each rotation

Mommy time

breakfast

chores

Bible: 20 minutes

Routine for multiple children

Mandatory stop at lunch time
(resume subjects next day)

lunch

read aloud

play/read/hobby for children

Mom rest time: 20 minutes

Mom works during children's
quiet rest

children play together while
mom works

dinner

evening routine

mom works after children's
bedtime

Mommy bed time: early enough
to allow for 7-9 hours of sleep
each night

Sample Routine:
Work-at-Home   see chapter 15

dad

how can you encourage him to get involved?

Get Dad Involved

More in chapter 15

- **Ask for advice**

- **Be honest with how you feel**

- **Tell him if you want help - or sympathy**

- **Tell him something good about the day**

- **Share academic progress**

- **Brag about a child**

- **Let children present reports to him**

- **Suggest field trips**

- **Ask him what role he wants to take**

- **Respect him and thank him**

No matter how much or how little he wants to be involved, he deserves gratitude: he makes it possible to homeschool; he helps provide for the homeschool; he lives with a tired, stressed-out homeschool mom; he keeps the homeschool family going. Those are big jobs. He is a hero.

working

What can you do to meet your own needs, your family's needs, your homeschool's needs, and your work needs?

Chapter 16
Special Children, Special Needs

symptoms

Brainstorm for a moment. What are all the symptoms you are concerned about?

maybe/maybe not

what are some special needs you think your child may have?

helpers

Who should you go to next for help? Who after that?

relief

What kind of help do you want most?

support

What friends, groups, and websites can support you while you support your child?

Notes

Notes

Notes

Notes

Notes

Also by Lea Ann

Homeschool Made Easy
Homeschool High School Made Easy
A Friendly Guide to Homeschooling (audiobook)
Rocking Ordinary

connect with Lea Ann at lagarfias.com

98306033R00109